antji
fiona moodie

fynbos fairies

English versions by Gus Ferguson

UMUZI

ARUM LILY FAIRY

Lend an ear to the Arum lily,
hear its silence, if that's not silly,

touch your cheek to the lily flower,
it's always cool, despite the hour,

dip your nose in the lily funnel,
breathe the depths of the deepest tunnel,

tap lightly at its yellow tip
to let, through your hand, a fairy slip.

Zantedeschia æthiopica

DISA FAIRY

See the little Disa girl
dancing by the stream,

swaying with the rushes,
washing her winglets clean.

She drinks, the little Disa girl,
dew from the silver tree.

That's why the little Disa girl
is so much loved by me.

Disa uniflora

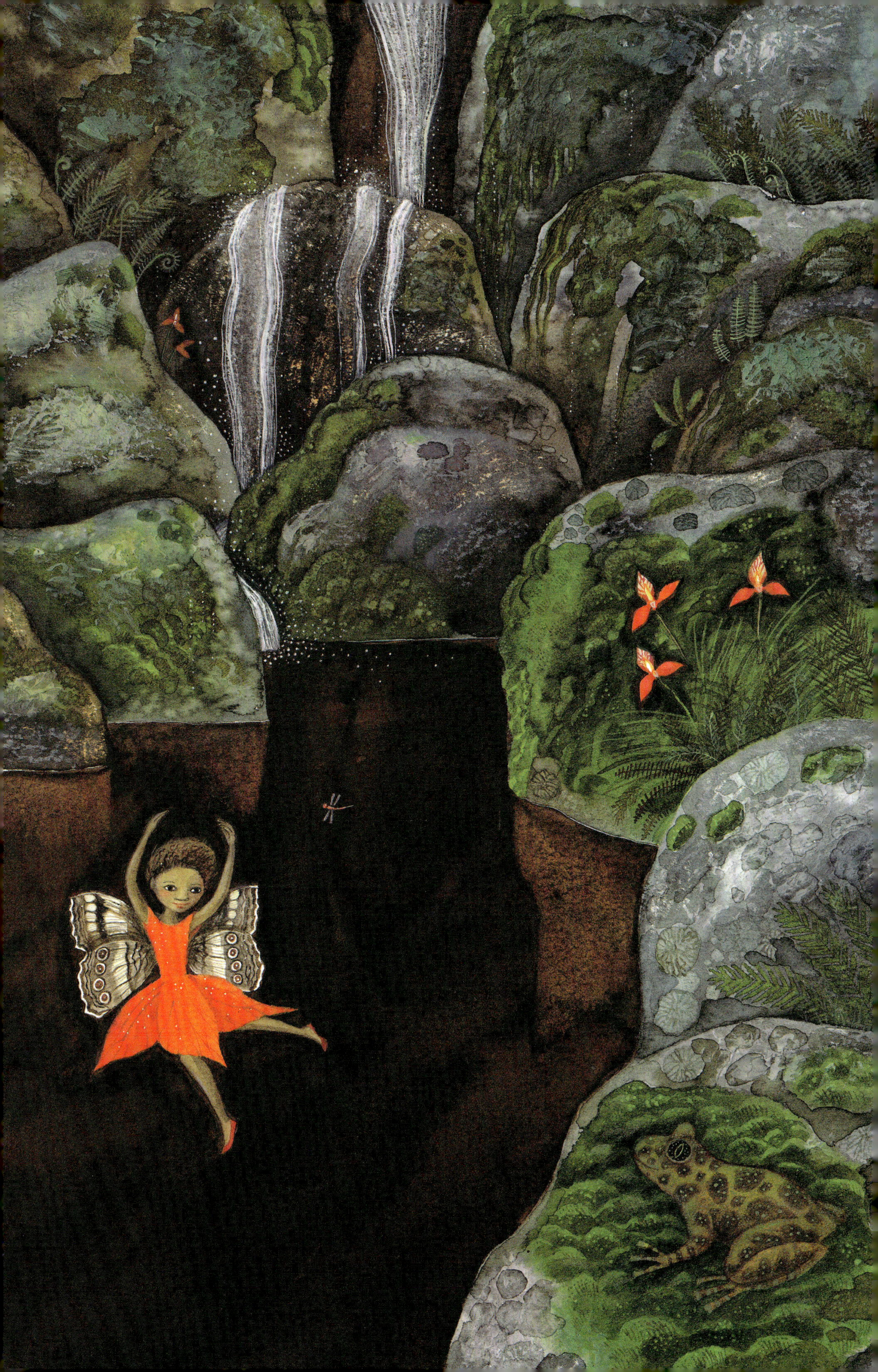

ERICA FAIRY

Come closer my darling,
look if you please,

see the wild-heather tresses
toss in the breeze.

Those red tufts and baubles
and lots of loose threads

are enough for the wind
to weave natty dreads.

Erica cerinthoides

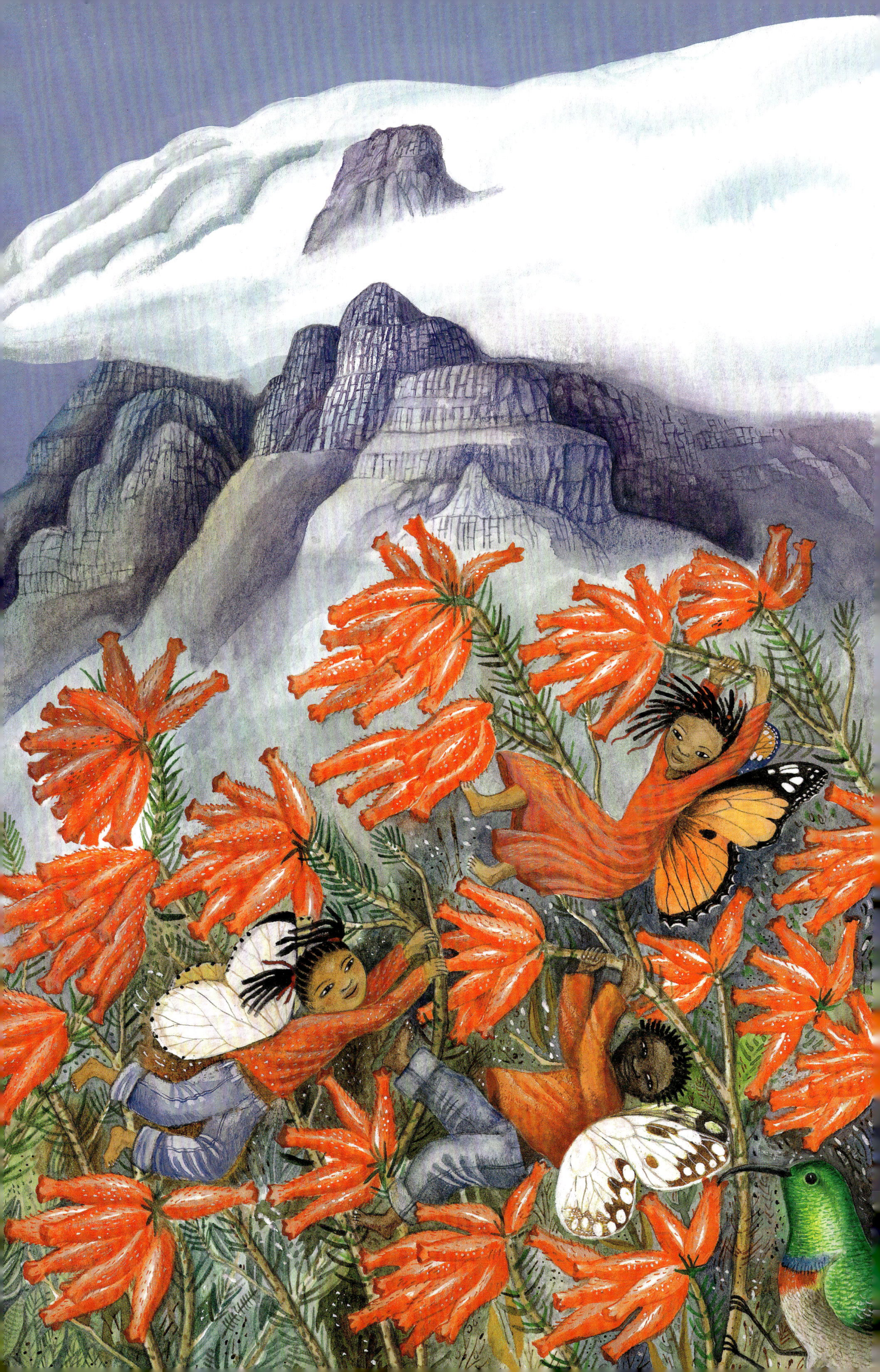

CHINCHERINCHEE FAIRY

When she swings her tiny tassles
your head begins to spin.

Her bulbs are filled with poison
but, her perfume pulls you in

and soon you're spinning short of breath
in a chinchin-chinning dance of death.

Chin-chin
chin cherinchee
chincherin-chincherin

o ch
o ch
o ch ch ch

Ornithogalum thyrsoides

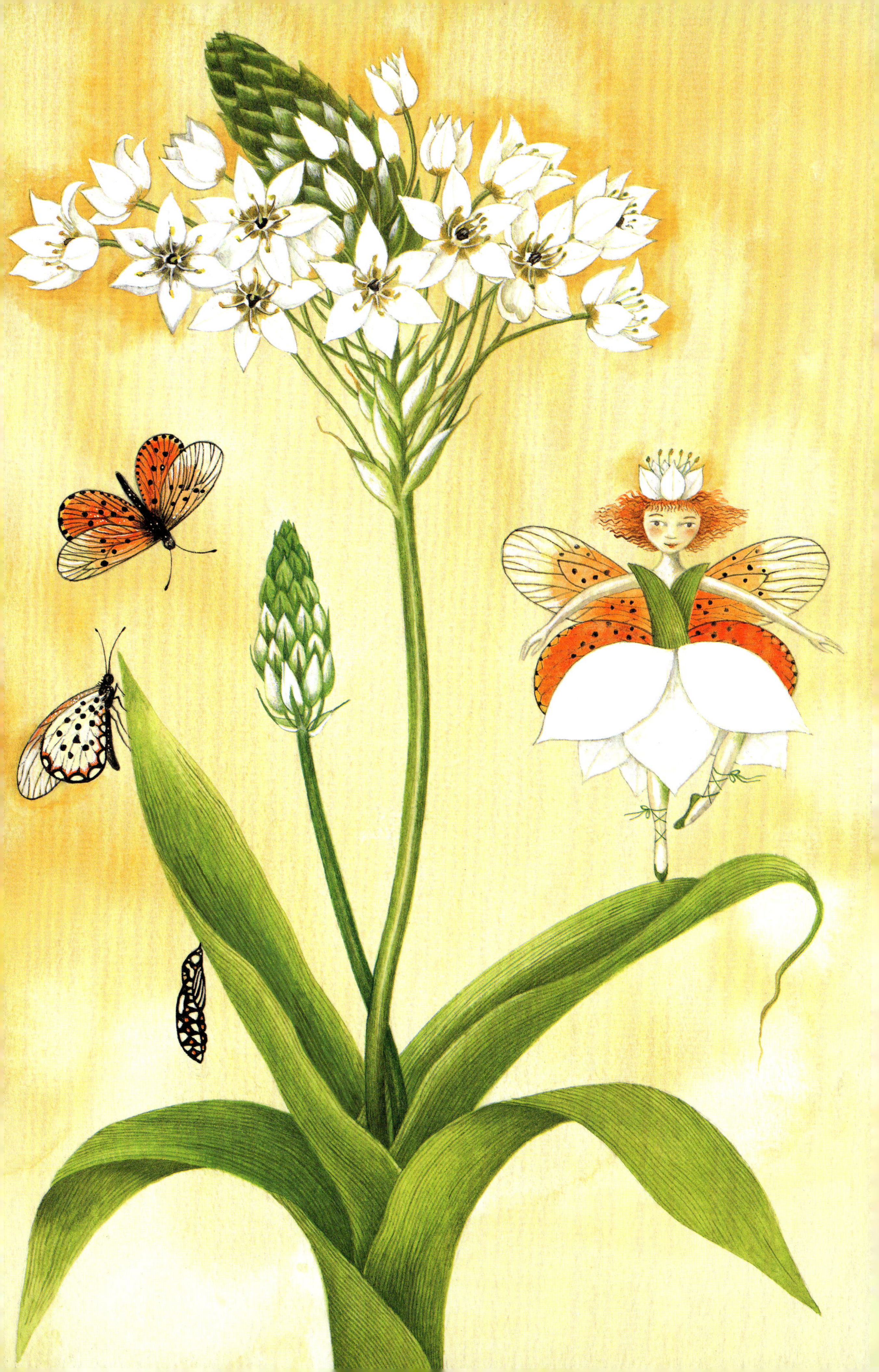

DEW-VYGIE FAIRY

All night long a fairy danced, danced
and danced herself into a trance.

And in the sickly light of dawn
was dizzy, sweaty and forlorn.

Then slow, beneath the waning moon,
collapsed on Vygies, in a swoon.

And as she fell some gentle bees
came buzzing through the shrubs and trees.

They knew exactly what to do,
they bathed her tiny feet in dew.

Drosanthemum hispidum

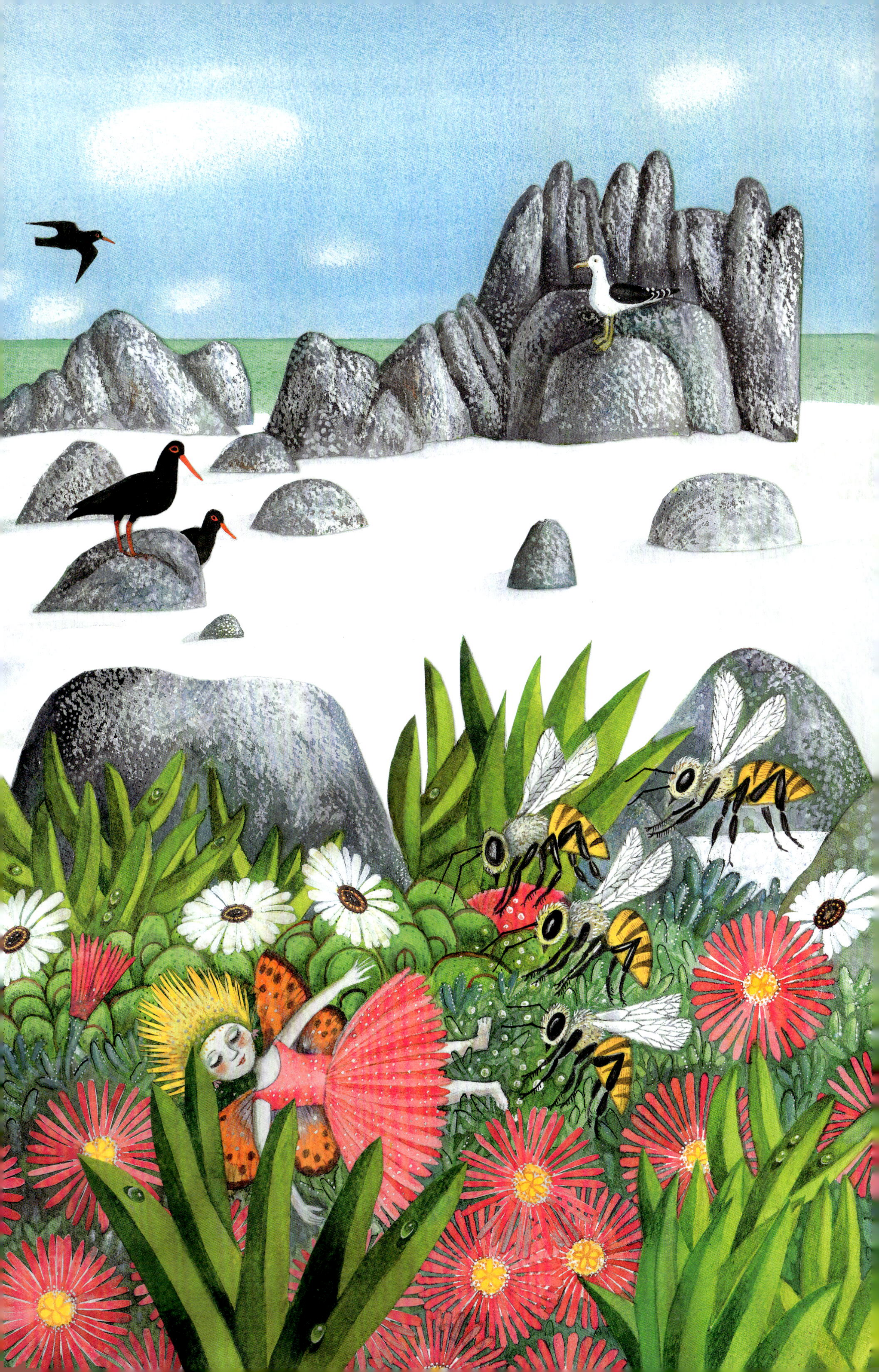

KING PROTEA ELF

The Protea elf in the protea crown
lazes at ease in the soft pink down

but he is the one who frightens away
the greedy white-eyes, he keeps them at bay.

Who slices through the sugarbird's tongue?
(so sad a bird should die so young)

Who nuzzles the King with his elfin lips
and strokes his leaves with their soft pink tips?

Who bays like a hound to sound the alarm
when bush fire crackles, breaking breaking the calm?

He is a protector, King Protea's knight,
a passionate warrior eager to fight.

"Without him," says the King, "I'm not myself,
I depend on my fiery Protea elf."

Protea cynaroides

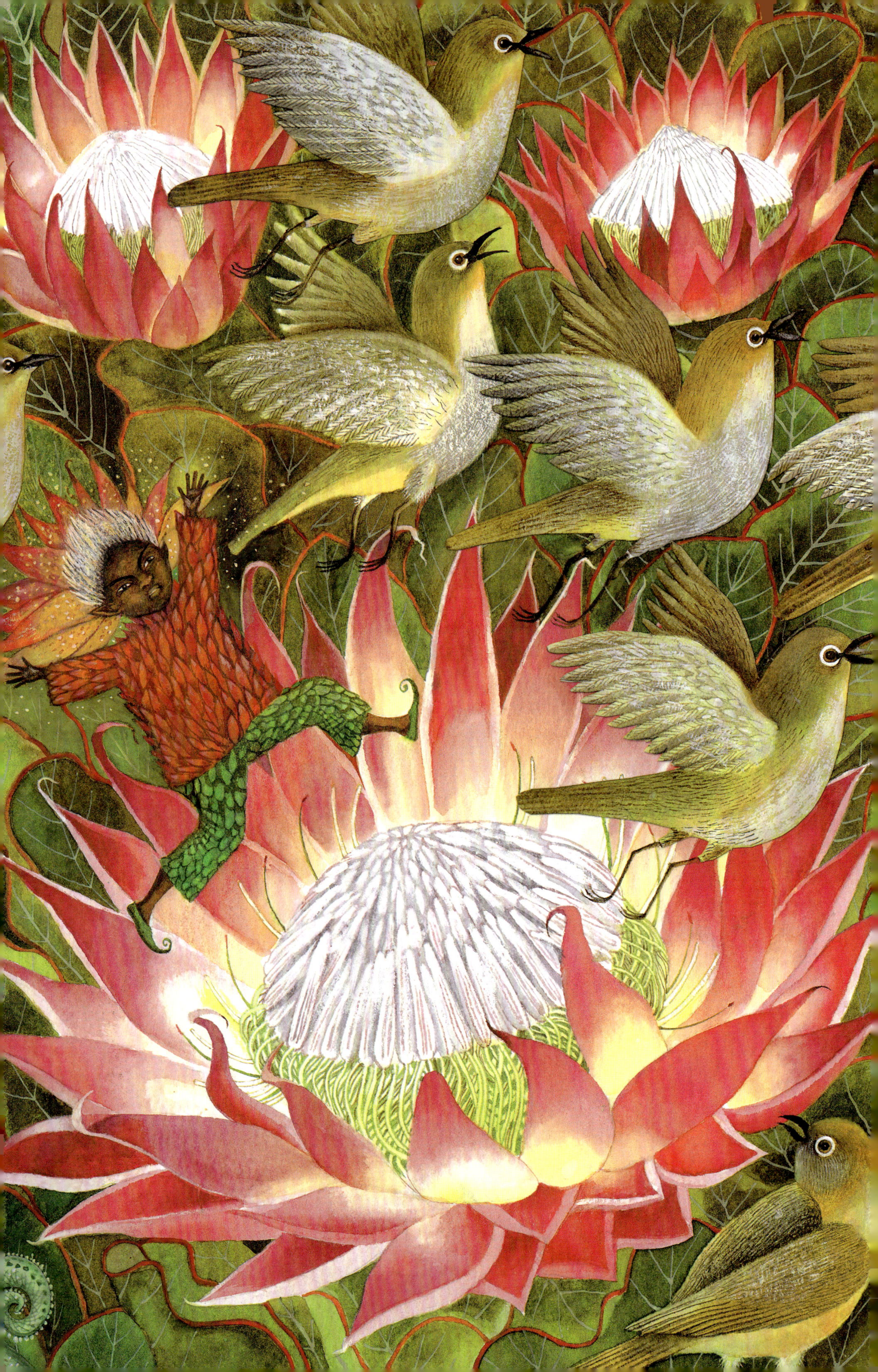

GERANIUM FAIRY

There is, of course, a granma fairy,
I wonder if you've met one yet?

For if you'd met a granma fairy,
she's someone that you won't forget.

Her eyes are sharp, her ears are hairy –
she is a scary granma fairy.

She smokes a pipe of malva-shag,
and carries a woodlouse in her bag.

Now come and rub a malva leaf
between your thumb and finger,

rub it gently, not too hard,
or else the smell will linger.

Then whisper, "Granma mama malva
ma malva malva mama malva."

Suddenly, kadunk! a shock and a start –
your throat falls down into your heart.

Pelargonium cucullatum

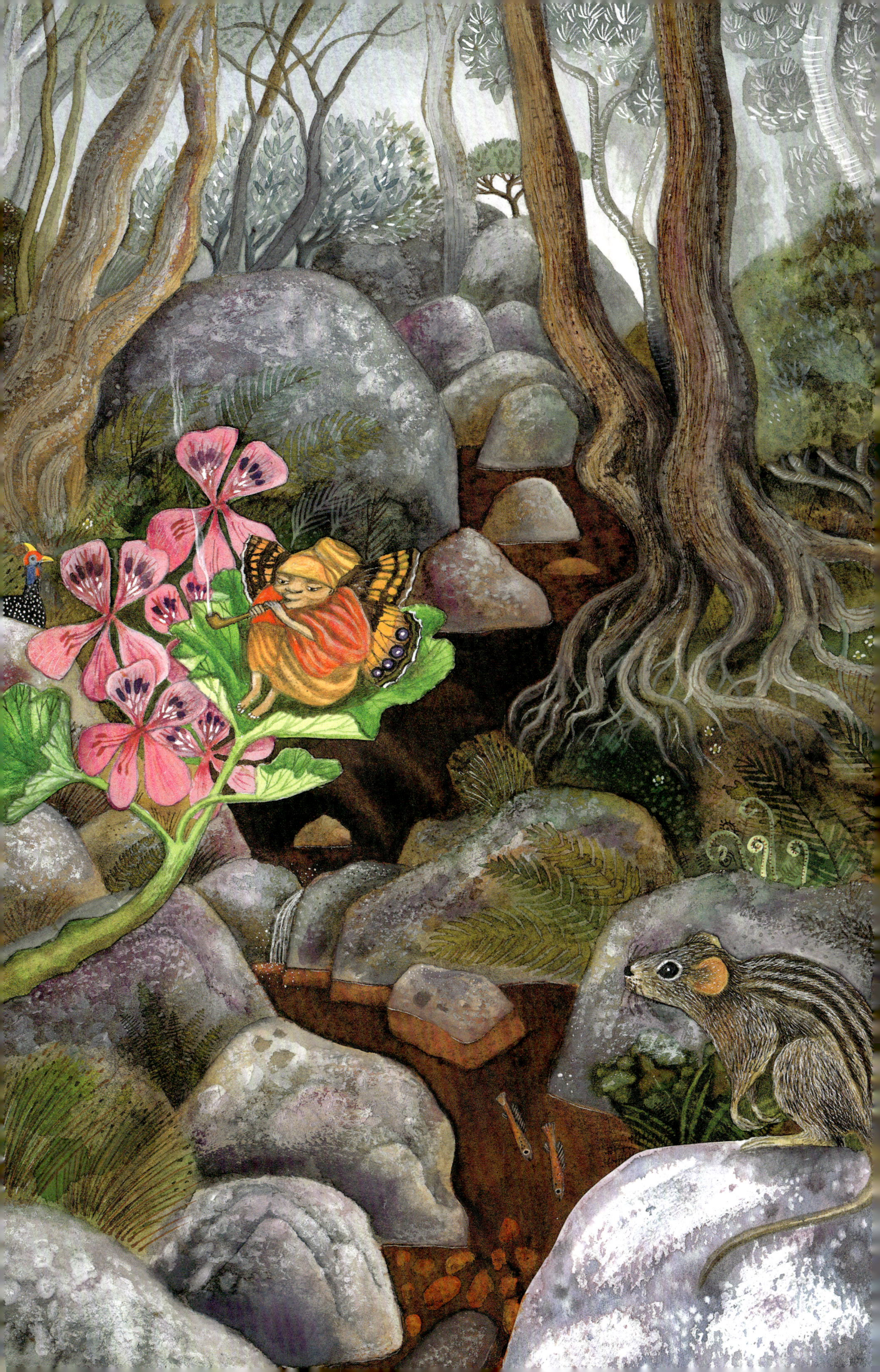

PINCUSHION PIXIE

See how the pins of the Pin pixie sheen
as she works on a dress for the Fynbos Queen.

She sprays the Queen's wings with honeybush tea
and perfumes her cloak with chincherinchee.

Then the Pin pixie steals the best silver leaves
from the branches and twigs of the silverleaf trees

and she stitches a frock that will shimmer and sing,
a glittering garment to please the King.

This morning the pixie pricked her thumb and it bled
and droplets of blood stained the Queen's dress red.

But lucky the Queen – who's haughty and vain –
didn't notice the blots or her seamstress's pain.

The pixie, embarrassed, gripped her sore thumb
till the bleeding stopped and the thumb went numb.

Leucospermum cordifolium

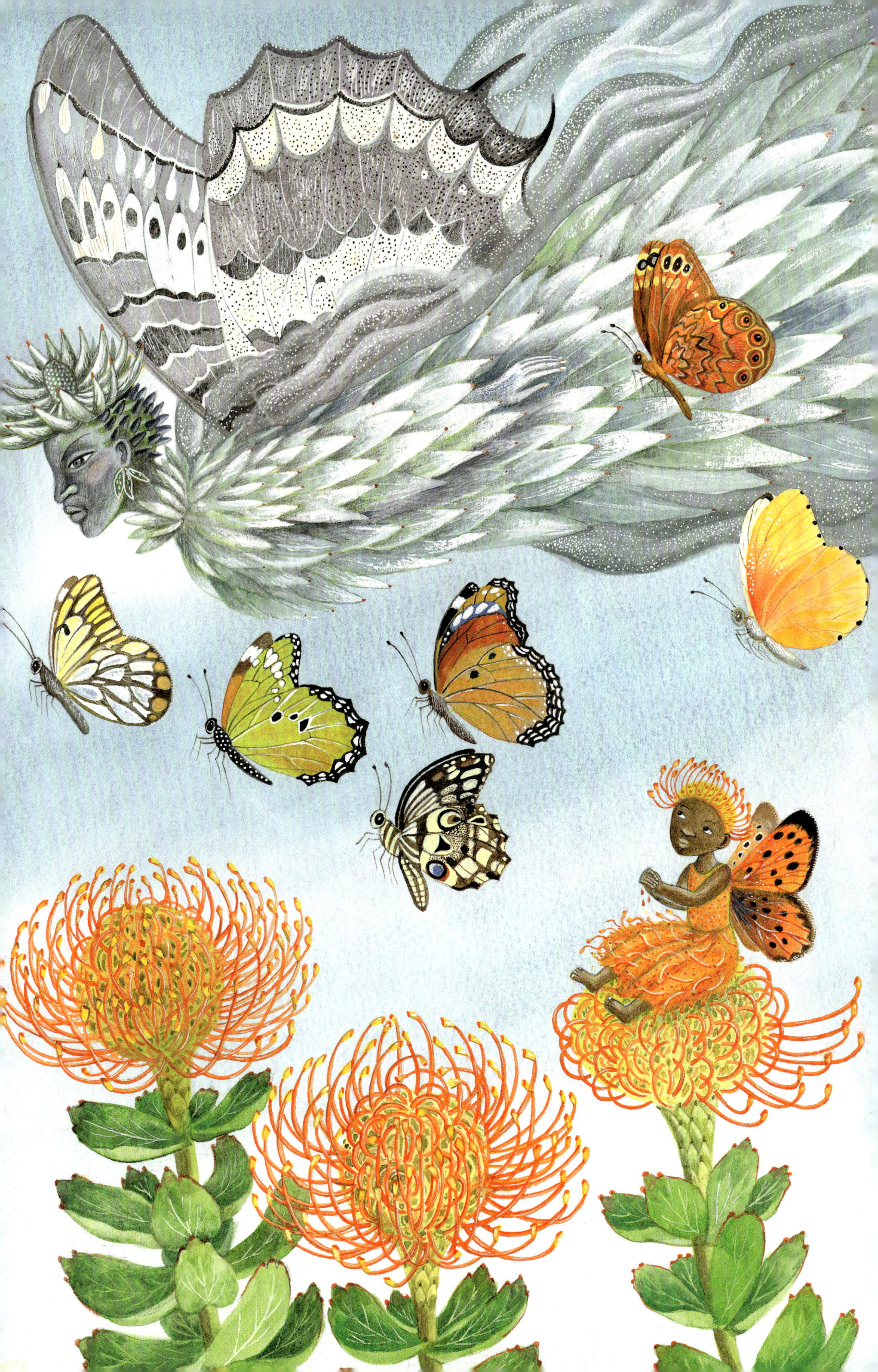

SORREL FAIRY

"Hey gently, gently," cries the Sorrel,
"you very nearly trampled flat
my little Sorrel big-bum fairy
who adds the sour to my sap.

She smells deliciously of goat's milk
and yawns continuously all day,
but when her funny bottom wiggles
I love my lazy, clover fay."

Oxalis pes-caprae

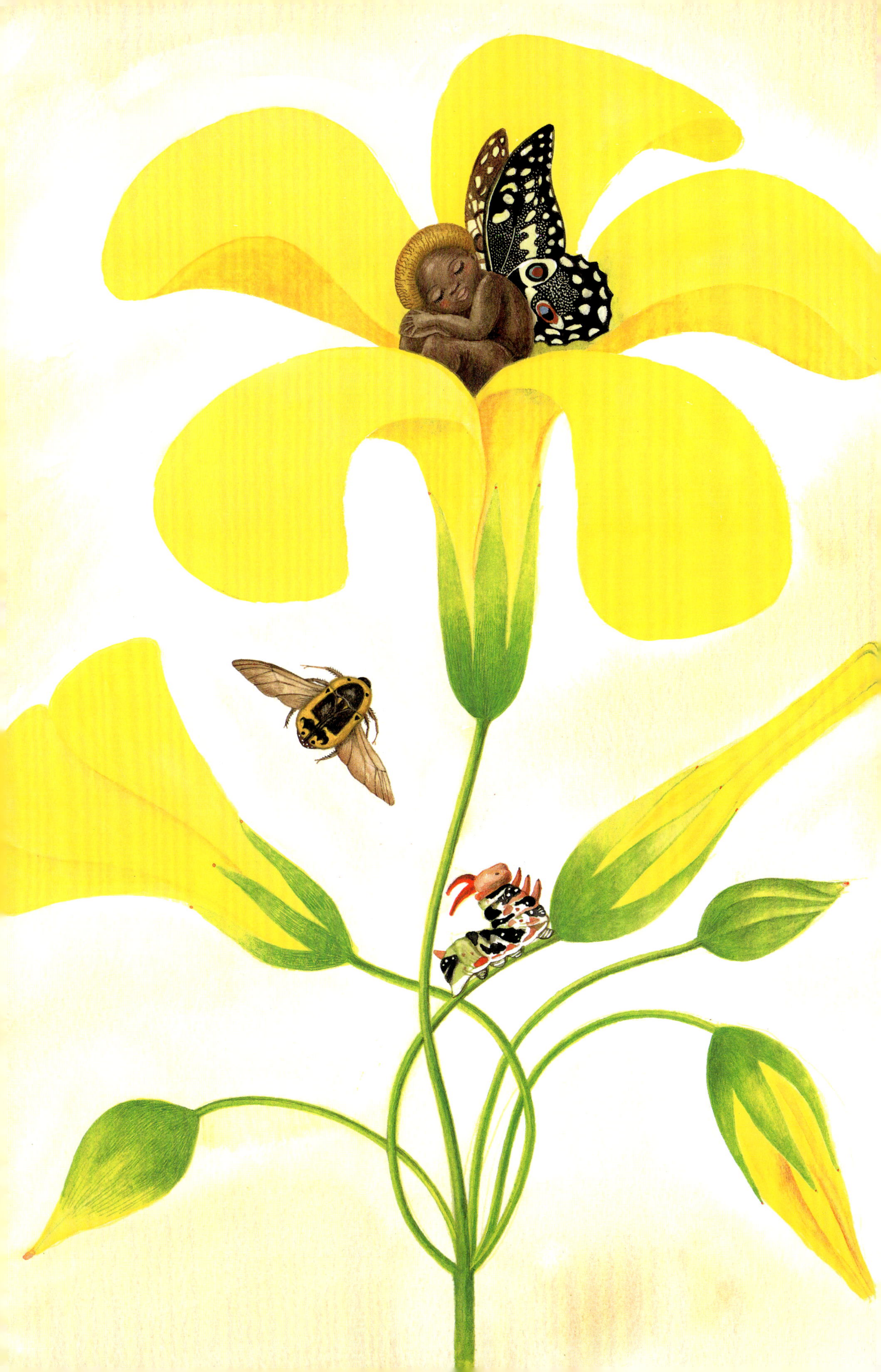

BUTTERFLY CLASS PHOTO

In the front sit Painted Lady and Common Dotted-Border
their winglets folded to.
You have their full attention,
they're staring straight at you.

Behind them Sorrel Copper
shouts to Lucerne Blue,
but blue boy doesn't hear him
as Arrow Head screams, "Yoo hoo!"
her feelers frantic in the air,
she needs to do a poo!

Pretty Citrus Swallowtail sits
and sips a cup of dew.

But shame poor old Grassveld Sylphy
is really feeling blue.
She cries, "You know what ugly Cabbage White
chaffed Boland who I love so true?
She said, 'Howzit Boland Skollie,
hoe lyk'it nou my broe'?
You know of all the butterflies
I'm the most in love with you!'"

Metalasia muricata

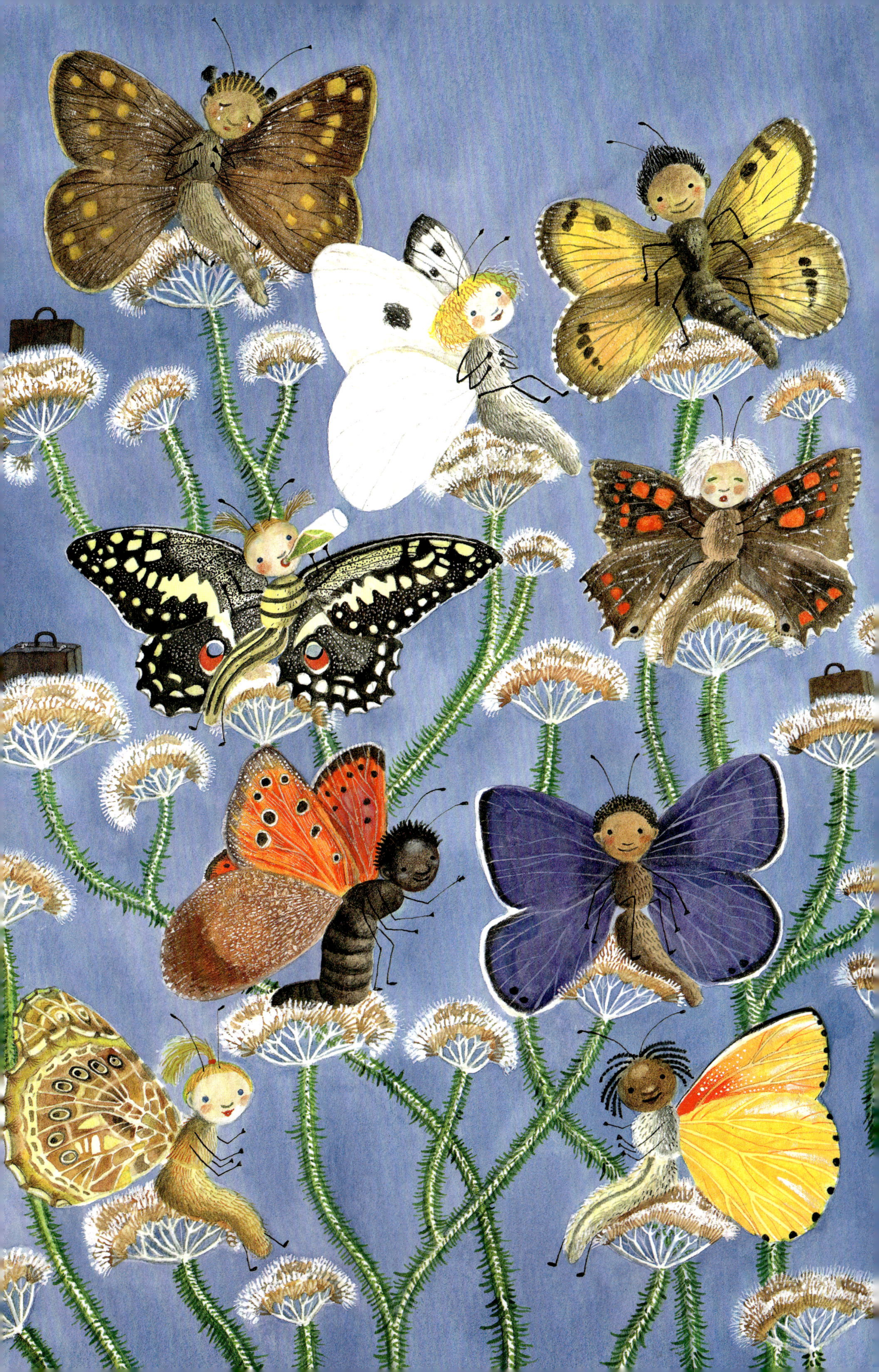

STAPELIA ELF

"Oh smell that foul stench of dead rotting meat!
I love it," said Horsefly, "my favourite treat!

I like it, I like it, I like it a lot,
that delirious stink of dead-meat rot."

"Then come," said Stapelia, "I'll show you the way,
I go there myself, at least once a day.

I'll climb on your back, my fine purring steed,
we'll vroom to the stench that's the source of your need."

Orbea variegata

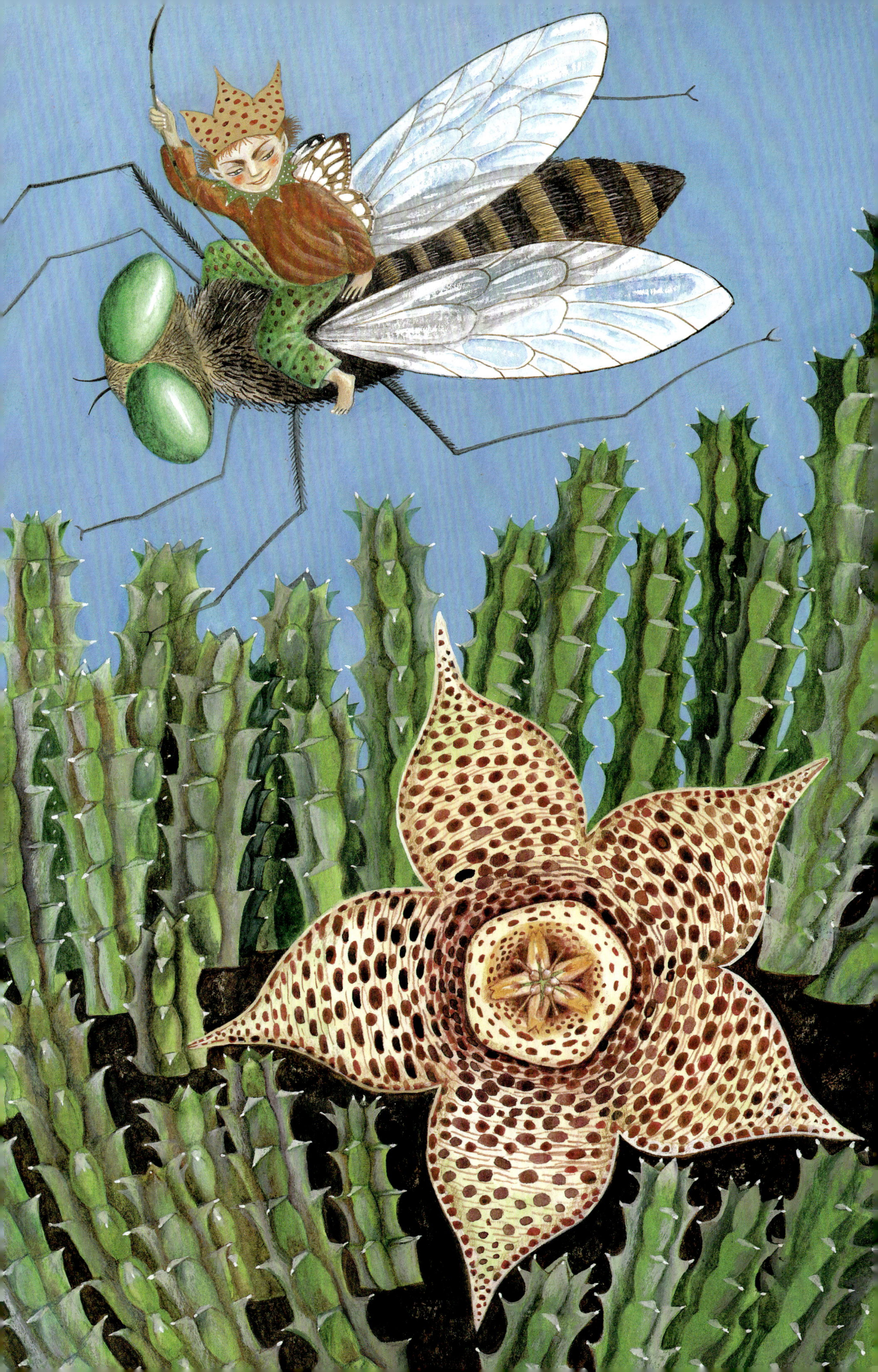

STRELITZIA DRAGON

Mum calls it a Strelitzia!
We know it's not! Instead

it is the wildest dragon-child,
flames shooting from its head.

HADEDA WITCHES

The Hadedas in our suburb sweep
like witches on a broomstick-flight
above our rooftop every night.

Now here's a secret you should keep:
their fearful cries that make flesh creep,
tell us these birds are scared of heights.

Strelitziaceae reginae

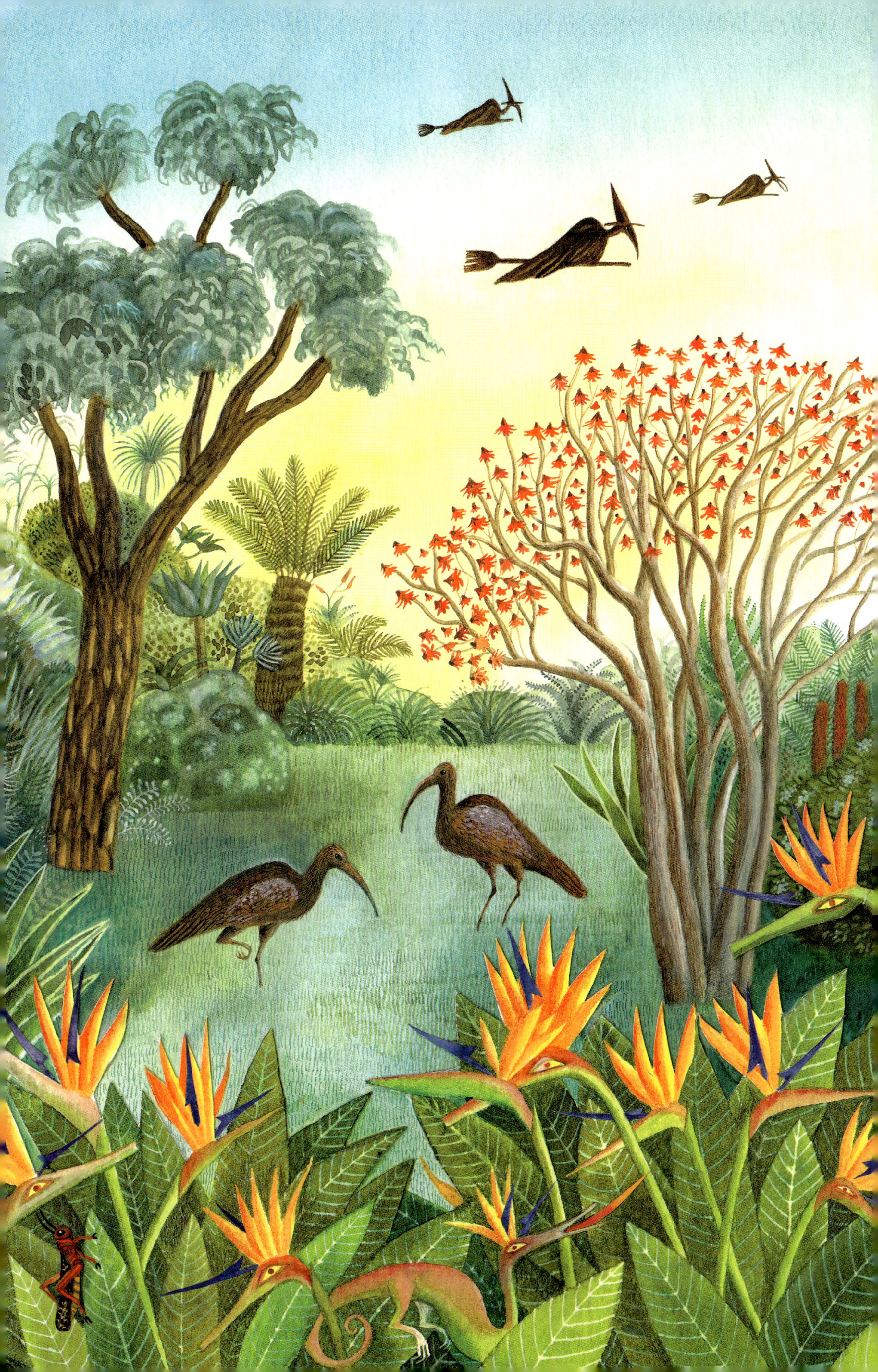

SUGARBUSH FAIRY

Lying outside on her tummy
she sleeps without a blink

while moonlight on a Sugarbush
glints silvery and pink.

Protecting her tiny body,
her winglets hug her tight

as something in the undergrowth
scritch-scratches in the night.

Protea repens

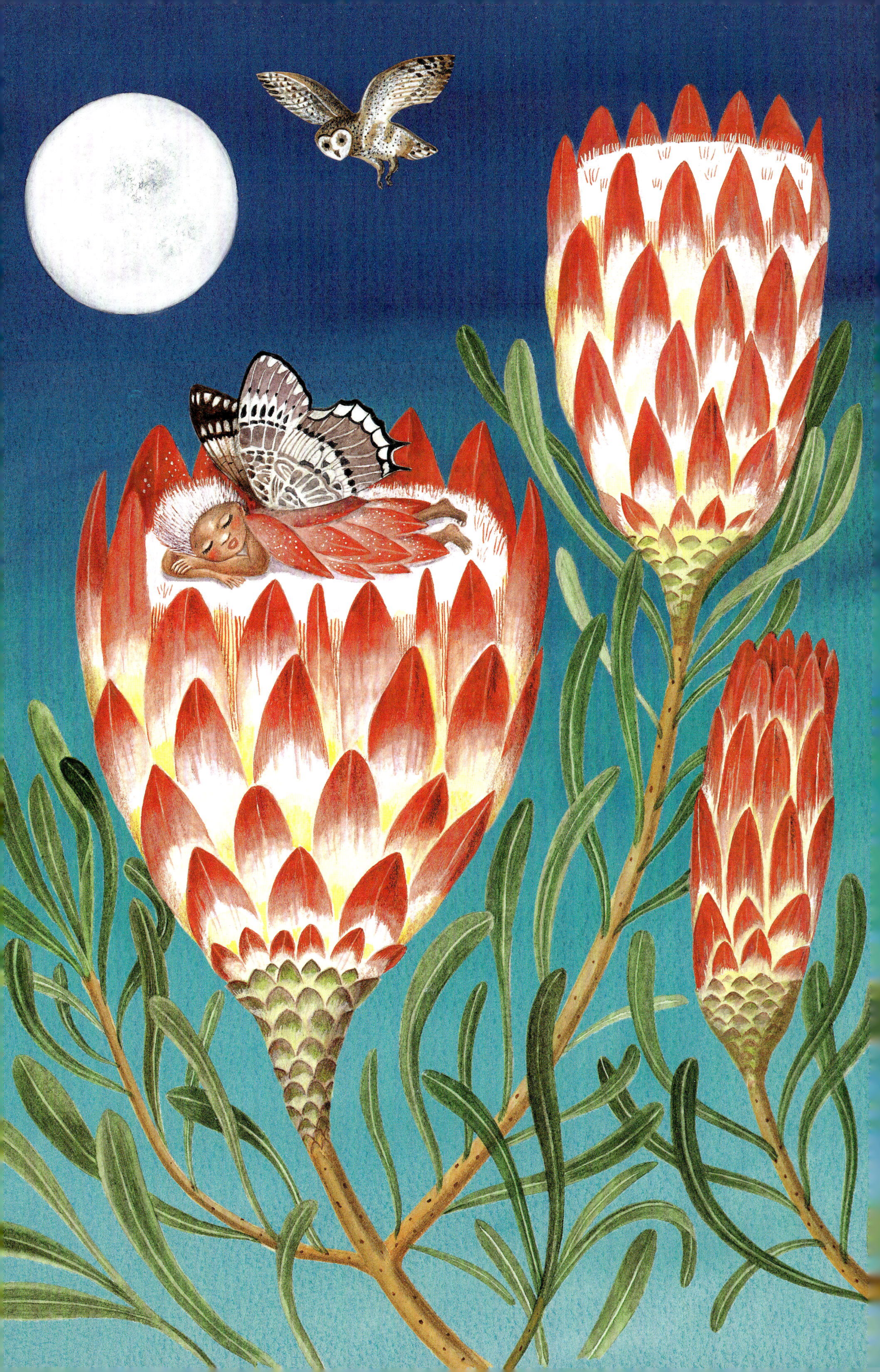

MILKWOOD FAIRIES

If you look carefully
you'll see them asleep
in the branches
of the Milkwood tree.

Back to back, snug in a cleft,
stretched on a leaf
they sleep but don't fall
from the Milkwood tree.

And if you look harder
you'll glimpse the moon
as it blooms and it bleeds
in the Milkwood tree

how it swells, how it shifts
from the earth as it lifts
as the fairies awake
in the Milkwood tree.

See their wings how they shake,
see how lightly they land
on the moon-white sand
under the Milkwood tree.

Sideroxylon inerme

WATERLILY FAIRY

When darkness closes in
the Lily-on-the-water moves

as moonbeams open up her fist
to find the nymph within.

Nymphaea nouchali

For Anna, who saw a fairy in the wild-plum tree, and for Clara, who didn't – Fiona Moodie
For Anouk, Antjie and Jana – Antjie Krog
For Tallulah, Luca, Ruben and Matteo – Gus Ferguson

The idea to link fairies to specific flowers was borrowed
from Cicely Mary Barker's *A World of Flower Fairies*,
which first appeared in 1923.

The botanical facts on the back cover are used
with acknowledgement of *Encounter South Africa*

Published by Umuzi,
an imprint of Penguin Random House South Africa (Pty) Ltd
Company Reg No 1953/000441/07
Estuaries No 4, Oxbow Crescent, Century Avenue, Century City, 7441, South Africa
PO Box 1144, Cape Town, 8000, South Africa
umuzi@penguinrandomhouse.co.za

Copyright in English text © 2007 Gus Ferguson
Copyright in illustrations © 2007 Fiona Moodie
All rights reserved.
No part of this book may be reproduced or transmitted in any form or by any means, mechanical or
electronic, including photocopying and recording, or be stored in any information storage or
retrieval system, without written permission from the publisher.

First edition, first printing 2007
Second printing 2008
Third printing 2009
This edition 2016, 2017, 2019, 2022
5 7 9 8 6 4

ISBN 978-1-4152-0903-5

Designed by Sally Swart
Printed and Bound by Shumani RSA, Parow, Cape Town